The Universe
at the Point of Contraction

Randall Dills

FUTURECYCLE PRESS
www.futurecycle.org

Cover artwork, Midjourney AI by Diane Kistner ("coalescing, universe at point of contraction, converging, stars, meteors, dark matter, fantasy, astronomy, muted colors, illustration, black lines, light --ar 3:2"); author photo by Angela Anderson; cover and interior design by Diane Kistner; Georgia text and Federo titling

Library of Congress Control Number: 2022951855

Published by FutureCycle Press
Athens, Georgia, USA

ISBN 978-1-952593-38-3

For Gracie Mae

Contents

Closed Doors at the End of the Universe

I.

At Snee Oosh Beach, where
the land is curved, carved
by a relentless rising sea,

the sailboat makes a run for the Pacific at Deception Pass,
a triangle sliding across the water.
You could push it over with your thumb,
knock it into the sea where your heart is,
filled by clouds, obscuring a ribbon of fingers
untangling, making space, fingers apart, unbridgeable—
we won't touch again.

What is there to do but let them fall onto your thigh,
your fingers—what they did, they won't do again.
The feeling rushes out of them, shaped in darkness,
midnight sky, torso turning, shoulder before head,
reaching for empty, arms unfolding
carmine satin rippling in wind, billowing, and behind it
the beyond, where

we were curious, but you slipped into the stream of life,
away from us,
our lips parted to form the sound of your name,
and we fail to make
all but a rounded
vowel, the mourning *O*,
and our lips forget your name.

II.

Do you recall that time in Wenatchee, above the Columbia,
the car door opened and the stars fell out
and with them my dreams for you.
You hung a foot out the door and went ashen,
looked back at me still in my buckle, the earth ripped open,
said,
You forgot my birthday.
I forgot all the birthdays.

And now, sitting in tall grass groping for ground,
triangles falling through the universe, looking for purchase—
What is below us? you asked in third grade.
That's a dumb question, the teacher says,

there's nothing below us, only space.
The girl says, *You see*
that sliver of goldfinch-colored moon, that's God's fingernail.

A tentative step on melting pavement,
on the hospital row,
a pathway between daffodils an honor walk,
the past shutting off like dead stars
scattering across a freezing universe—
the last time you shut a farm gate,
the last time you pulled a coffee cup from a cupboard,
the last time you stood silent in a crowded room—
memories like birdsong at dusk
as the tree line goes from pink to blue.

The earth is falling—
we walk through doors
you'll never come out of,
one foot, then the other,
through a dusting of lemon-yellow light,
limbs angled,
acute, obtuse, acute,
falling.

You understand.

I see it in your eyes.

Hospitality

Eyes shut tight against you
one day in March, morning
full of monsters and teeth gnashing
and *thump, thump, thump:*

You ragged thing.
You tenderfoot.
You do not have to fight anymore—
come gently, inch by inch, curl
your bared bones
back into me, kiss feet
kiss hands   kiss tears
and swing low. We go down
in a field of lilies—
seeking hospitality—

This is my body and
it is for you.

Mountain Jam

In the foothills
on the banks of the Sauk River
a band with a fiddle,
a collection of misfits

hunched over *gitars* and *mand'lins*
playing the old dead masters
from the 1970s.

Between songs,
talking about how they died,
about how a tree turned to stone,
about that ol' knocking sound of an engine cooling off.

The rhythm of that porch-stomping mountain 'nanny echoing down the
valley back home
in Cartoogechaye.

The banjo picker saying,
The thing about me, is'm always thinkin' 'bout leavin'.

Them old men left those major chords in the forest.
They come down the mountain, the last of the old ways going.
Said to their lovers, *It did sound good now didn't it.*

Silver River

In twilight on Fontanka
I gaze at someone I loved; it's a fever dream.
Mayakovsky wants me to read his old Soviet poetry,

it is before *glasnost* and I am a patriot,
so I won't.
Anyways, he's a futurist and

I feel the past again and again
walking in step with ghosts.
He hands me a black and white photograph

in which he does not smile, and
soon I will sell it in souvenir stalls behind
The Church of the Spilled Blood.

The poet says love is not required of any man,
not even Rodchenko, who only makes my frame
and loves in a Constructivist way.

I
fall,
silently,
into a silver river,
it is dawn, and I am dying,
Mayakovsky's last letter on my mind.
I am loved, and loving still.
It is a small test of endurance;
a tiny revolution,

to live.

And so I do.

Pretty, Pretty Self

Do not despair—
you've been here before,
you know the way to your
pretty self

You, always with your pretty, pretty self

Tell the gods your plans, you say,
And what are yours?

Live and let live
a little farmhouse with a riding mower.
a warm little farmhouse lit up with lamps in winter
a place to read when
rain lashes at windows,

a row of cypress trees to last a thousand years.
For them to call me by my proper
name.

A life for me
among ruins.

Old Dog

In the high country north of the Sauk headwaters below Glacier Peak,
he lay there looking on stars,
wishing he could name just one,
wondering why now of all times and places
he could feel the earth,
feel the heat leach out of it,
feel the vibration of her voice coming on wind
carried across leaves of yellow cedars and noble firs,
dissolving across the alpine meadow,
where it fell just short of him.

He called forth in his mind a lifetime of her muted fragments and
      phrases,
a whole life trying to speak,
and the fleeting moments
when the light caught her face just right,
after she chose silence.
How often they looked at each other's turning shoulders.

Next to him, three embers of a fire remained.
Orange mountain juniper gathered starlight.
Old Dog nuzzled up against him. Old faithful.
Loyal Old Dog, digging in, knowing what comes in the night.

Wind Carries Water

Wind carries water
in through the window
where you dwell, sleeping,
        stippling
the words of poems laid aside,
cracking them like granite,
pooling inked memories:
this touch, that silence,
that finger on this skin
          on those
late summer days, and
makes space
        breath,
makes space
        silence,
an arc traced,
sorrows whispered.

The edge of awakening:
a chest heaving as a
rising sea at storm gives
itself to the wind.
The wind.

The wind.

A Farm, One Morning

In the farmhouse a half mile from the county road,
the one where they didn't get the hay in this year,
the one with the barn leaning into the ground,
the one with lead paint cracking:

What is it the rain strikes at night
to make the sound of earthquakes, a
thousand tiny tremors rippling through
bone?

Why does the rooster crow at dawn
to pull me from slumber, bringing back
the specter of a day?
A dog bellows at the door.

From a tin roof water falls,
bends the petal of a pink rose,
pooling in red clay, the white seeds
of a black cottonwood float
misshapen, like a memory, so much so,

you come back to me through leaves of grass, barefoot, wet, broken.

Muck Boots

The dawn came blue on the Salish Sea.
On Fir Island Road, there is a mannequin
tied to a telephone pole.
A black stallion gallops along the fence in the field by the road.
A man pulls over, rolls down his window and
yells, *I love you!*
    In the stable a woman sings "Amazing Grace"
    to an old show horse called Patriot.
    You can see its ribs now,
    so it won't be long.

At home on the farm,
a woman tugs on her
muck boots
and says to her husband
as he makes the coffee,

I don't like the way you live.

Stolen Orchard

Between two arms
of the Salish Sea, on
a farm cut from forest
near the old fern prairie
where Samish women
gathered camas bulbs, there
is an orchard at rest.

Ringed by a sagging fence
of barbed wire, blackberry bramble
and verdant spring bracken.
These apple trees and
these plum trees in
this orchard at rest,
this life-giving trespass,
this resurrection—

      Last summer
the fruit spoiled and
fell into tall grass.

I was tired, having
lived in the world
of my own creation
every waking day.

This year when the time comes
I will open the gate
climb the ladder and
take fruit in my hands.

Two Summers Ago on Fidalgo Island

I.

The finches have returned to the farm. The sweet peas are in the ground. A girl falls off a horse. The horse circles back around while the child lies on the ground crying. She gathers herself up and leads it by the reins to a tree stump. She grabs the bridle and knuckles its flank to turn it around. Rain begins to fall. She climbs into the saddle again and goes straight to the kick, and runs it hard across the pasture at a gallop toward the barn. Somewhere a screen door slams.

II.

The birds stopped trilling.

The child comes awake in shin-high grass and dandelions. Nearby a goat chews at fiberglass. Bulls in the pasture lock horns near a bathtub turned on its side. The child kept fish in there until the raccoons got them. A horn honks, *Go home,* a voice calls. She watches a caterpillar climb a blade of tall grass, sees it go still as it bends back toward the earth. She goes back to sleep.

III.

In the forest, she says,
I saw the bear yesterday.
There ain't no bears here, he says, sitting next to her on a log,
knee touching knee.
I s'pose one could swim over the channel.
It's a long way from mountains.
Not too long.
There's a lot of eating between here and there.
I ain't seen no deer around here either.
Coyotes got 'em I guess.
What do you know about coyotes?
They come out at night, sleep all day.
So nothing then.
I don't worry about coyotes.
What happened to all the deer then?
People.

IV.

The clock ticks.

Wet clothes sit in the dryer.

A child opens a door and peers out of darkness at the people assembled in the dusk. Her family, her aunts, uncles, and cousins. Voices echo and turn corners, but she can't make out what they are saying. A cow moos, a dog answers. Everyone laughs. Sagging paper sacks of apples, oranges, and bananas sit on the porch. She leaves them there and shuts the door, afraid.

V.

A gust of wind rattles a black bucket on a fence post. She hears the sound of hooves pounding earth. Two riders on horseback emerge from the forest, a mother and daughter, the mother calling out, *Fire!* The forest is burning. Smoke streams skyward. It is visible on the mainland. Cold saline water laps at the shore. The ferries run empty across the rising sea.

In the Graveyard of Volcanoes

Off Snee Oosh,
on a farm gone ramshackle,
upstairs in the sickbed,
he listens to the rain
come up island off the bay.

       A specter saying to him,
What do you know about farming?
You got no sense for it.
But that's the way you want it.
The way the wind roars here
you'd think—

In the pasture
the last horse, the Bashkir Curly,
attacked by mange,
rolls in dust turning to mud,
hooves in the air, head lolled,
looking for the shed, blinking out rivulets.
There's nothing to be done about it.

The first day of spring:
pooling in the depressions of the earth,
the unbearable darkness of rain.

Mama's Hands

At the farm off Gibralter Road:

Mama, Mama, she cries, *your hands!*

It's okay, youngin', she says. *It's just from finger-pickin' and chord changin'.*

Her mama pulls her close, lets her feel the texture of her hard, calloused fingertips. *So that's where music comes from,* she thinks. She rubs her mama's fingers for a long time, thinking about all the notes and songs still inside her, how she might get her own songs out through her skin.

In the orchard, the apples begin to fall from the trees. Hawks squawk in combat above the pasture. The filly bolts for the stable. Mama puts boot to board, taps out a rhythm.

Cottagecore

His grandparents were country people. He never learned much from them on account of having his ears closed off to any ideas that weren't his, seeing as how he thought he knew everything. And so he was helpless. His sister carried on some with the old ways. She had a vegetable garden and did some canning, and pulled fruit off the trees for jams and pies. For his part, he bought a book about country living at the Farm and Ranch store. The teenage cashier had her hair in pigtails and braces on her teeth, but she'd been farm-raised. She looked him over and said, *It's a little late for you, don't ya think?* Being sensitive, he read the book sparingly.

One Night Out West

There is water in the fields where the sloughs used to be, before the dikes and levees and the Great Fill-In. Alongside Memorial Highway, there's a whole river underground, surfacing, forming lucent pools of reflected, ancient starlight. The islands glow fluorescent in the distance, across the flats, over the strait, beacons for my father who set off walking this winter night in February. It is a long way to the potter's field, to lie down, to let the earth take him. With lucid memories of every farm and fence post that used to be, he says, *this used to be an ocean, this used to be a glacier field, there the Swinomish used to fish. The settlers came here for grain and grain boats came from Pennsylvania. It was in all the papers. Mount Baker and Glacier Peak, one day they're gonna blow.* And my father says, *I can't do this alone.*

The Last Days

The hottest summer on record.

Before an A-frame beach cabin on the Strait of Juan de Fuca, she sits under the sun, cross-legged, drinking water from a canteen, droplets leaking down her smile lines. Sailboats idle in the strait, waiting for wind, reflected light from spars signaling secret messages to the uninitiated on shore. She watches butterflies, a shimmering fortunate few, the last of the luminous orange Checkerspots flitting above beach grass, coruscating like tiny distant explosions. She worries about the volcanoes—the ash might blot out the sun, the lava drown us in hellfire. She turns, runs into the cabin, screen door slamming, echoing, rousing the Great Dane, whose dolorous howl, like a fermata, drifts, and drifts, and drifts, over ocean spray—

57 days without rain.

Watershed

1.

As the sun peaks over mountain ridges and the light stretches westward, land falls away beneath it to the coast. The sea is dark and everyone sleeps but her. She takes the teapot off the boiler before the whistle.

Since she arrived in this place her feet have been in every creek and stream in the Skagit watershed, and her ankles bathed by the Salish Sea. They called it by a different name when she was young, and by another name before that, as some still do today: *Whulge.*

2.

He appeared at the kitchen door.
Did you sleep all right? Did you see the meteors?

She said, *I dreamed of chasing butterflies through Celtic ruins on a bluff in Portugal; and of the time you played* Rubber Soul *for me over the telephone.*

3.

The porch swings in afternoon light.
The cat sits at the screen door.
The hummingbirds have come.
They flap their wings and float backwards.
The child asks,
Have you ever seen one?

4.

Near where wildflowers grow among outdoor antiques,
she examines a willow carefully;
It's been two years since she planted it.
He is silent, watching from the deck as shade falls across his face.
Below, she reaches up, up for a catkin and pulls.

5.

Evening ends. The porch swing, empty, rocks to and fro. Inside, they sit at the kitchen table, with coffee. *What are you thinking about?* he asks. She says, *My friend who won't come home...and about the time I saw the Salish Sea lapping at the rocky shore.*

The Junk Lady of Germantown

In Germantown, where every three months people
set out junk for the city to haul away,
a revenant appears on the streets
wandering back alleys with
some rope and a handcart.
She appears listless to some who see her, as if
lulled by heat and
the rhythm of wheels turning over aged and rutted blacktop.

Every now and again she is pulled from the charnel house
of her mind's eye
with a jerk.
A wheel stuck in a hole.
Asphalt washed out by pounding rain after a morning deluge.
She is alive and
rubs her reddened hands.
This she can feel.

There is nothing she cannot do—
but heal.
It is not up to her,
she is not living in a time of her choosing.
But to see her take something old and
make it new again
you'd think she'd been touched by a higher power.

The trucks come along behind,
loop around her as
she bends and wrenches the cart free.
Vultures on the first pass.
Men with lit cigarettes in mouths,
carrying their calcified bones in bags of parched skin from cab
to curb.
Engines idle; they
toss aside what was once revered.
They are looking for scrap, she knows,
but they don't know how to make something out of nothing.
And so the spoils of the trash heap fall to her.
She sifts through the discards—
a sideboard, a child's rocking chair, an end table bleached by the sun.
She moves slowly and takes her time.

In a tar paper shack off Schiller Avenue,
behind the house with all the lights on,
the one near the cemetery,
she sets to work.
She folds the paper in three
as air cools in luminescent light.

It is in the doing where she marvels,
amid steady tempo,
where past and present reach concord.

If you've heard the sound of a hand sanding on wood grain
or felt roughened fingers on greeting,
you have known her.
She performs her work well.
The only pause comes when a screened door opens.
A voice calls and the past begins again:
Mother, won't you come inside?

The Left Ear of Father

There is no escaping the noise my father makes. A cacophonous, dissonant clamor roars out of him. There is sing-song, scat, whistling and cat-voice: *Kitty-come-now, get some lovin'.* I hear him when I am out back reading. In youth, I considered his commotion noise pollution. Why won't he stop? He's deaf in the right ear, and spending life on his right side, it is the one into which I used to speak. There was nothing there to make me heard and so I stopped speaking to him and grew into resentful silence.

When she was alive, I asked my mother, *Why is he like this? For a long time,* she said, *there was no noise.* He could hear only the refinery and its Cat cracker and the vitriol of hard unhappy men until he tuned out their calumny and grief by going deaf. *Now there is noise,* she said, *the noise he makes. It means joy, it means he's happy. When I made amends to him, I spoke to the left ear and through that ear, he hears me still.*

Great Grandmother at Similk Beach

She met a man who
in his youth charged a bear
and lived
taking her hand as if
he had always been waiting to greet her again
amid driftwood, whole trees preserved

in death. She stands with him
in stereoscopy, stitching together,
something new to grow
beautiful in that place,
Similk Beach,
where the Skagit and the Salish come together,
there is no sign of her but

unspoken memories and
the things she touched.

They say the few people who
go to Similk Beach today
like it for the solitude.

Matrilineal Line Cycle

1. *Grandmother*

What remains of the matrilineal line?

Of grandmother,
there is an upright piano
and a bench at Echo Hill.

Inside the bench are hymnal books,
sheet music with notated margins,
taped to cardboard cut from old cereal boxes.
Her taste ran popular, all rag, rhythm, and Sunnyside.

I did not know I would want to remember her and so I have not.
I saw her only when she was old and in a home.
Fingers frail, interlaced in her lap, even the phone ringing
to announce her death rang true, on Christmas morning, 1981.

If I wish to have of her what she wanted me to have,
then I must learn the staff and play,
feel her vibrate
through my inner ear
in two-four ragtime.

The rest, she keeps.

2. *Mother*

Of Mother, there are a few things.
A box of recipes for sugar-free baked goods from the 1980s.
Substitute Apple Sauce.
Substitute carob.
A scrapbook, dated 1994, marked
MISCELLANY.
She would sit at the table
sipping Kahlua, pasting
clippings about what men said ailed her, the thing
that was in her:
Body fat.
High fat diet.
Sweet foods.
Sipping, pasting,
Trick your body into losing weight without dieting.
A letter from TV's *Low Calorie Gourmet.*
Pages and pages of
obituaries: Age 45. Age 48. Age 34. Age 36.
Age 50.

Donations
may be sent to the
American Cancer Society.

Page opposite:
a wanted poster for a con man
who stole her checks,
washed them carefully, and cashed them
at the small-town bank where she had been
a customer for 32 years.

A page of photos of her ideal version of self,
thin, blonde. 1965 and 1966—
two good years.

She sits,
sipping, pasting, not hearing me
say words I never spoke,

You did not do this
to yourself.

3. Daughter

Up on Echo Hill,
in a cabin sheltered by towering Sitka spruce,
among elder kin in coffee klatch,
she sits in light that yellows her hair
in front of a piano built five generations ago.

She fingers keys with ease,
finds Middle C,
listens to the vibration,
hears the tone and presses again,
two or three keys at a time,
and it sounds like music.

Clusters of notes filter out
through open windows and
blend with the sound of water
smoothing rock in the creek bed.

Among her kin, these keys bind her
to the gathered spirits.
She clears her throat.
We pause, cups at lips.

Three Photographs of Mother

1.

I think my mother wore blue all the days of her life. It is hard to know for sure because she seldom allowed herself to be photographed, but in the photos I do have, at least the color photos, she is dressed in blue. I have a handful of photos of her, most of them collected after her death, one or two from each decade of her life. No one knows the through-line that connects the dots of these pictures. I'm not sure she wanted me to know. She never spoke of the past to me.

Yet, she liked to fix herself in time. There is a clock in some of the pictures. Five o'clock. Half past six. A quarter past seven. She had an acute sense of time. When she was sick and found my attention irritating, she'd look at me and say, *I am not going to die tonight.*

2.

There is one photo of my mother at a house on Beverly Park in Everett in 1947 or 1948. She is three or four years old. She wears what I imagine to be a blue button-up sweater. Her hair is tucked beneath a blue bandana. She is perched on a newly built fence. She refuses to look at the camera. There is something out of frame drawing her gaze away. Did her father speak in Polish to her? To try and get her to look at the camera? One day she startled me by saying a few words in Polish. When I asked for more, she said it was all she knew. She never mentioned it again. At the time, I did not know anything of the Poles in Ukraine, in Terebovlia, or what might have happened to them. The links between me and that language, that history, are severed.

3.

My mother is in the Cascade Mountains on a spring day, holding a chunk of icy snow. How did she get there? Who took the picture? She might have had a free day and headed east with friends on Highway 2 to the mountains. In later years, she did not like to go out. She is not looking at the camera. She is wearing an open button-up sweater and jean shorts. She long wore that style of button-up sweater. Why? She liked the pockets? We were always finding wads of toilet-paper, tissues, paper towels in them.

I go to the mountains more often than she did, but I like to stay home too, in the woods, on the farm. I still wear an old blue zip-up hoodie of hers, pockets stuffed with paper towels.

4.

In the early 1990s, she constructed a family tree. She wrote letters and
sent them to Appalachia, Canada, the Great Plains. She solicited stories
from aunts, uncles, and cousins, near and distant. It was grand in scale,
numbering over a hundred handwritten and typed pages, reaching the
edge of the family's living memory at around 1900.

But, for one line, she's not in it.
Kathryn L., b. April 6, 1944–

Later, someone completed the sentence in blue ink:
October 6, 2007.

She is a mystery to me. Her silence is intentional and eternal. She gave
me what she wanted to give, and what she gave cannot be touched. Did
you ever hear her laugh? When I remember, I pass it on, and she lives.

The last photograph is the only one where she looks straight into the
camera. My mother stands in the center in her blue sweater, arms
hanging at her sides. Before she died she told me that this was how
she wished to be remembered. She knew she was dying and wanted
the photograph to be displayed at her funeral. We looked high and low
for it. We looked in the attic, through scrapbooks and old photo albums.
To no avail.

Years later, across the country, when unpacking boxes after a move to
Kentucky, I found it in an envelope marked "favorite pictures." I was too
late. Now there is nothing but the shape of grief on the bodies of those to
whom she gave skin, the shape of mouths clenched tight against truth,
the shape of hold it in, the shape of before and after, the shape of you
had a mother too? Yes, I had a mother too.

Zh-ch-sh-shch

There was a light mist over the Skagit valley this morning. A red tractor idled in a field below Bow Hill. It rained all through the Chuckanuts. There was a rainbow at the top. The eagles kept to their nests. On the radio the CBC broadcaster out of British Columbia spoke of the *dog days of summer*. And suddenly a memory. Driving out of Champaign on a humid, sticky, summer morning. Up I-39 to Beloit College. Across the Illinois river bridge at La Salle. Over the Kishwaukee and up the Rock to study Russian in Wisconsin. Trying to form the sounds that come in so many Russian words: *zh-ch-sh-shch*. It was a long time ago. The first summer after my mother died.

Thud, Nine Years On

O, these many years I have carried
the memory of sound waves captured,
called back and fueled; it's
ressentiment:

What cruel sound is made when
mortuary workers drop a body,
a mother's body,
on rain-slicked pavement?
Thud.

There is no other sound like thud.
It comes on like thunder
nine years on,
thud.

Incurable and racked with cancerous tumors
she was incomprehensible in her final hours—
the sounds that came out of her, unintelligible,
until there was
peace, peace, peace

and she was my mother again,
as if she had just awakened, in contemplation
of a day she might live again.
This I could deal with, remember, or
forget about, or
explain away,
but not that goddamn thud.

Southern Exposure

Outside a farmhouse
in the southern exposure,
where the line between pasture
and lawn is obscure,

two people sit in chairs
sinking in the earth. So much air
in the world but not enough air
to say what needs saying. Tall grass,
a gate ajar, a feral cat, camouflaged,
hunting cottontail.

A pair
drinking coffee,
coffee in throats,
coffee cups breaking
apart.

It's always
the leaving
and never
the staying.

It did not have anything
to do with fists or words
or heat: just an unspoken
thought that came in the later part
of an afternoon after a wide smile
after a sly comment that revealed
these two knew more of each other
than any other living soul,

followed by a note,
and a going.
The kind of going
familiar to itinerants,
people of the road,
people of wandering spirit,
but

for those who
come home to find
things emptied,
things hollowed out,
there's nothing
except hurt,
so

maybe you turn on the tap
maybe reach into
the ice box and
set some meat
out to thaw,

maybe open the cupboard
and marvel at its disarray,
begin to stack one can atop another,
lining up the labels the pretty way
like you like it.

Waiting on a Woman from Kentucky

Coming from back east,
heading west for the coast
waiting for her in a car

buffeted by the wind
on a South Dakota backroad
off US Highways 12 and 83.

She's made the acquaintance of
two women in a red truck.
Women she's never met before.

I can't hear what they are saying.
There is a lot of gesturing and laughter.
It's the same story everywhere we stop

I haven't spoken to anyone but her. Still,
if it takes a long time to reach the coast
because of moments like these,

I will be satisfied, happy.

Washington Haircut

My hair grew long in the
six months and two states
between cuts.

It touched my shoulders for the first time in my life.
I liked it, but
could not keep it off my face,
out of my eyes, and so
did not see many things and

ignored so many simple solutions
The barber said,
What a mess.

At my last cut, I had a
house, job, wife.
That was in *Ken-tuck-ee.*

The new cut revealed
     a bald spot, one white hair, and a patch of grey
     and none of the other things.

How to be a human among humans when
in retreat from this world toward other distant worlds,
and have someone say
feel this touch, do you recognize it?
To shut eyes against it and open upon a new day, where

from a low bed, I remember everything ever said to me,
watching stars become the yellow finches of morning.

In My Father's House

My possessions:
books, 12 boxes
Long Play records, one box
record player, one unit
smart phone, one unit
cheese, one pack, sliced
pastrami, one pack, sliced
    This food is high in protein
mementoes, two boxes
    From:
        —Russia, a matryoshka doll
        —Portugal, one Meadela scarf
        —Germany, one tin pin, "Reichstag: Besuchen in Berlin"
        —Mexico, one handwoven bracelet with national colors,
"Mexico 2009"
Trinkets from dead people.
    From:
        —Ellensburg
        —Champaign
        —Huntsville
        —Louisville

Faces who scream at me across the cosmos when I am tying a shoelace,
saying, *take it, this is for you,*
when washing dishes, scraping baked cheese off a plate with a jagged
        nail,
when my daughter looks over my shoulder at an image on my phone and
        says
Who's that?
Who scream at me, *answer the phone!*
Scream at me, *touch someone!*
Who scream, *live!*

Exes Drive North and Talk Boxing

Prologue

Outside King Street Station,
there was a man on his hands in a garbage can,
a poverty-proof can, cemented into the earth, so
you tip the man, legs bicycle,
a man has needs, and

I need things too,
I know the feeling, how it happens,
you are up to something,
concentrating, and suddenly
your body is in an unnatural position,
blood rushing one place or another, fight or flight,
how do you run when your feet can't touch the
ground?

Act 1

She is on the train coming north out of LA.
She'd been in LA to sing, one foot from stardom,
eighty degrees and palm trees and
homeless encampments and
then it was over. Three minutes on stage
and a tattoo.

The tattoo:
Float like a butterfly sting like a bee.
The artist met Ali in Vegas
when he was eight years old,
when his sister got married,
when Ali was there for the
Sugar Ray Leonard fight. They
rode the elevator together,
September 16, 1981.

All the signs were there,
read the tea leaves,
draw the stars in a pattern, divine water
in the footsteps of children at the motel pool,
heel, toe, bob and weave, it's rope-a-dope,
O Fortuna on Route 66, the gods of
Pasadena that swallow voices, but
mark the skin, in three acts.
All the signs were there.

An antique shop, section 7,
beneath the blinking fluorescent light,
a bee vase on a stand with a line of sight
to a butterfly shirt, next door,
in the tattoo shop,
drawings of bees and an artist named Honey,
float like a butterfly sting like a bee,

Ali, a woman on a bus tells her,
was from Louisville, Kentucky, *same as me,*
and so is R and that makes three,
Float like a butterfly sting like a bee,
all the signs were there, cosmic, or
a comic's punchline,
Float like a butterfly sting like a bee.

And then she's on the north train
and I'm coming south, both of us
going two different directions toward
a single point in time at King Street Station.
It's a story problem.

Act 2

Seattle.
Beneath the Venetian campanile,
King Street Station, 2nd and Jackson,
the guard says.
Are you waiting on a train? Says,
You look like a man who'd stand on his hands
in a garbage can.
The war of the body has no victor.
I have a car and a job and a cottage,
but this body, the war of the body is
over, a long period of reconstruction
lies ahead. I say
Yes, sir, waiting on a train.
What's it called? Where does it originate?
Quick, quick, quick:
The Empire Builder, The City of New Orleans,
Southwest Chief, Sunset Limited,
The Red Arrow, The Peregrine Falcon,
The Orient Express, The Palace on Wheels, *it is*
The Starlight, sir, outta LA.
10-4, he says, *So I won't see you again next time 'round?*
No sir.

She comes off the train,
two days on the train, two days of
the conductor saying *Don't cross the tracks on smoke breaks,*

two days for him to know her, two days for him to peg her as
a wanderer, a dreamer, a seeker, someone to watch,
to keep this side of the tracks.
We used to be married.

Act 3

I carry her bags,
put them in the trunk with hard hats,
tool bags, the repository of broken promises,
busted dreams, rock bottom. We have an hour
in the car together. I lied: *It's not my car.*

We are talking about our daughter, we two who
met someplace in deep time and have this daughter,
this child of the cosmos, this star dust, this being
that floated to our feet on a feather.

Halfway and we are in a drive through.
Dr. Pepper no ice, no ice, no ice, no ice, no ice.
She sings, *this was the day that the Lord made,*
but her voice is gone, she dances in her seat.
*They gave me three minutes, but maybe
I wasn't meant to be on TV, what if I was there for
float like a butterfly, sting like a bee?*

*It's so dark, do these headlights work,
are they gone?*

We drove over the bridge to the islands.
She doesn't know the names of the islands but
she thinks they sure are pretty and
God shows out for me, she says
her flat top, her piercings, her tattoos,

        it's cosmic.

A Year in the Life of a Tall Man,
Citizen Science Data Point

A tall man
in the railyard full of
overgrown rust-encrusted train cars,
walks with purpose, stalking
Old West ruins looking for shelter
strength, sustenance, life. Tall,

everyone remarked
how tall he was,
an intrusion in every conversation.
You are a tall man,
where'd you play ball? He says,
I am. Nowhere.

He was cliché, a stereotype, typecast,
threadbare coat, stocking cap,
but some people loved him,
came to him, talked to him,
tried to get him off the street.

He combed through the trash and
found a burrito from an American
taco chain, still in its wrapper.
Warm.

He rode the bus,
had a gray beard, cliché, a
stereotype, typecast
but that's how it is on the street,
He had been sober for a while and
he liked to go back to the meeting hall
every now and again,
see his friends and drink coffee.
Shiver in his seat a little.

Origin Story:
It's cliché, he's a
stereotype, typecast.
He quit his job. No plan.
He thought things would be better:
It couldn't get worse, right?
But that led him to the railyard.
He slept in an abandoned train car,
he pulled cold aching bones
in and out of the car until
someone else claimed it and sold the space

reproducing world-conquering capitalism
backed with pure American muscle, it's
cliché—

He'd been something in his past,
earned a bit of money and recognition,
he never played basketball but
he once wore a white suit and
stuffed a black kerchief in the pocket and
attended a gala and gave a speech,
well-received, made the rounds, slapped the flesh,
but then it was all gone, and someone asked,
could you sleep in a cardboard box for one night?
Stereotypical.

A charity comes around and
hands them out, boxes, but he never takes one,
doesn't see how he'd be comfortable in it.
The first night he slept in a yard behind a fence and
got rousted right away. *At least I'm not in the woods*
he thought, but then he was in the woods,
a nice spot in the city,
undeveloped, way up in the woods, but
still in the city, hard trail to get there, an obscure trail,
but he found it, a nice spot by a stream
and this was a good place for a tall man,
a tall man among tall trees,
typecast.

He knew it was wrong to pee in the river,
to evacuate his bowels in a bucket and
dump it in the stream, effluent, punishable
by fine if you are incorporated, but he was
not, how could he be? A single, tall
cliché of a man, stereotypical, typecast.
That's how they caught him;
he'd turned the water turbid.
Some do-gooders downstream tested the water,
trying to make it safe for salmon, he'd seen the stencils
on drains, "Salmon Stream, No Dumping, Drains
to the Sea," but he was one, solitary man, hu-
man, a be-ing.

A lab ran some numbers and
there was an anomaly and downstream,
in the city while he slept,
there were interagency discussions,
a sector identified on large map on an
oak table, coordinates plugged into a computer,
a drone deployed.

It rained,
thumped on his bucket, slicked off his tarp,
got his feet wet, for he was
too tall,
a cliché, a stereotype, typecast, he
listened to it rain, and then he saw
heads bobbing up through the bracken
hacking, the police, with a social worker.
They found him, they were so loud—

      asking if he knew about fecal coliform,
how it got in the water from the way he
was living. *Do you understand?*
You're killing the fish.

The social worker said,
Come in from the cold.

The Sound of Dimes

M, off the bus out of Denver,
back from Kazakhstan or Tanzania
or Brittany, hear now on
Muhammad Ali Boulevard, hear now
city come to life, borderland breathing,
hear, now,
the susurration of voices rippling across 9th Street
swirled into silence in the eddy of waters
pooling around drains after late summer rains.

Listen, M:
Welcome to Louisville.
There's the Mayan-Cohenesque fusion restaurant
on Frankfort,
cochinita pibil to try, and
raking sand in the Japanese Garden.

Your muse, M said,
can you see her,
can you feel her,
can you draw the famous blue raincoat?

I said,
She still has her eyes,
but I can tell you
nothing else of her.
The last I saw was darkness,
a handprint fading from the hood of a car
and after that:
the pay-phone,
the sound of dimes
falling through levels to the
change box below.
The muse says,
why does it always have to be me?
She says,
to thine own self be true.

Imperialists Waiting for the Bomb

Long before we parted ways,
we met at 11th and Skagit, 1983,
in the schoolyard with a view
of the islands in the sea.
We'll go there someday, we said,
before the world ends.
We laughed and
waited for the bomb.
We thought we could hear tanks and
the hiss of a missile but
Red Dawn never came.

In the time of the War president,
I went to Russia to serve as a prophet and
you rode a dusty bus into Chiapas.
When it broke down you took your shoes off and
walked barefoot on the side of the road.
You wore a bandana to disguise your identity,
but I still saw you on the BBC,
behind the voice,
the hologram,
the figment.
His Mayan cause won your heart before
ex uno plures,
long after we parted ways.

Bundled against the brisk wind from the Gulf of Finland,
I stood on the balcony in Piter,
smoking for the first time in years.
I hoped for a posting to Cairo, or
that they'd listen to my phone conversations with Natalia,
where nothing is ever said, and
revoke my passport.
Later, in a quiet moment in the Moscow embassy,
the attaché leaned over and whispered,
They watch you.
An academic, hair thickened with pomade,
cleared his throat at the podium:
*It's a moderately authoritarian regime with an entrenched security
        force.*

The last I heard,
from a friend of a friend,
you were in Phnom Penh on mission
while I was still heading south, ever south,
struggling to learn Spanish,
getting stranded in the Sonoran desert

among a sea of saguaros and
The Queens of the Night,
waiting among *coyotes, polleros,* and ghosts,
waiting, among traces, fragments, and desperate footprints,
waiting for the bomb.

Life Among Strangers

For DK, 1980–2017

Fort Worden,
Friday night,
on the Quimper coast
of the Salish Sea,
a little shy of midnight,
with strangers gathered for retreat in
the dormant Ring of Fire.

We are at the old battery down on the beach.
Long ago the military commanded the heights here,
but for a few days,
it is us spiritual folk.

Like aliens at a distance,
with headlamps and flashlights,
climbing up and down three tiers of the stripped down,
decayed battery,
staggering through tunnels,
leaping from hidden passages
scaring each other, screaming,
convulsing with laughter.
There are giggles in the darkness.

Up top, two dozen people lie down,
bodies close on cooling concrete,
making patterns out of stars.
It is clear and stars are close,
just beyond outstretched fingertips.
More stars emerge from the darkness
silencing peaceful bodies connected to a deep past
of everything that ever was,
where you turn to your neighbor, and
grasp their hand, a squeeze that says
I am glad for knowing you, and
it feels real, the kind of peace we seek.
But we are fearful of being happy,
it might last forever.

No one says anything for a while.
We stare at the past made light.
A collective gasp erupts
as a shooting star crashes
across the atmosphere.
Someone describes the true nature
of shooting stars and ruins it.

The myth is gone,
but beauty remains.
A man reads from an app
telling us everything we can see:
Cassiopeia, Neptune, Uranus.
It's always funny and leads
to a lot of sex talk.

We lie there
listening to the sea
come ashore.

Living, breathing,
quiet creatures,
and still.

The moment passes;
we grow cold, distance reclaims its
space between us.
You want to give everyone a hug
but propriety stops you. We

climb down,
pile into cars and head up
the hill to our beds,
strangers,

the last time we gathered in that place.

On San Juan Island

I go to American Camp,
but not English Camp,
tip-toe among red foxes
to the scene of the Pig War.

In the lighthouse at Lime Kiln
the docent teaches me
the principles of the lighthouse keeper.
Say "station," not "house," she says.

She dares me to lift a five gallon can of kerosene.
They used to carry that up a ten-rung steel ladder.
I bent to pick it up and she says, *No, don't.*
You'll hurt yourself.

I stepped into the Haro Strait, where
the sea is expansion and contraction,
heart and lung
from time immemorial.

You once rode a bus a thousand miles for me
but now, when we know what we know,
We can't speak of it to each other.
I bend to the sea and weep.

Plague Ever After

It is about loss,
      piles of driftwood at Similk Beach
      decaying, cement-encrusted boots
      the calderas and the volcanoes
of the Pacific Northwest.

Bare feet on cold floors,
about searching for the beat,
little tremors of the earth.
About lost dreams, lost childhoods. Dead rivers,

the plague.

Elbows in the grass, the turn of a head,
criss-cross applesauce, hands folded in a lap.
The spinning tire after the bike is laid down.

It is forgetting the feeling of limbs in motion,
in flight, flying,
flying
up a gravel road
across a pasture,
toward home.
to you.

We don't remember what we want to remember.
Instead it is

      sitting on a tarmac with the seat belt buckled.
Flying a kite at Gasworks Park on the shores of Lake Union.
A voice on a crackling international phone line on
Christmas morning

      the tone of a phone receiver off the hook.

That one summer, you know the one, with its oily
grime on a neck, the aching inside that comes when
you are in bed and hear a car door close. It is
crossing the border from Finland into Russia with the sun
at your back. It is learning what hospice means.
We wait for the front door to open

bringing a memory to unstop the dam that keeps
one from looking back and feeling just
how it was, with you, who
are gone.

Notes from a Series of Lectures on the Skagit Watershed, in a Classroom and in a Creekbed

—Susan Wood, Biologist, Padilla Bay National Estuarine Research Reserve

The biologist said,
Can you hear photosynthesis?
It is a mudflat hissing.

Phosphorous, there's no gaseous phase.
It flows down river to the ocean.
The salmon bring it back in their bones.
When they die after spawning they feed the forests.
Optimum temperatures for salmon incubation
are 2 to 6 degrees centigrade.
Juveniles and adults thrive in water temperatures
of 8 to 14 degrees centigrade.
Anything higher is dangerous.
Conifers are better creators of large woody debris
needed for spawning.
This wood lasts fifty or sixty years.
Alders and cottonwoods are more common,
but they decay faster.

Why are fish dying in the Salish Sea
before they get to the open ocean?
Why is the Salish Sea a death trap?

We don't know.

Postmodern Biology

The story of our postmodern life is
measured in the sea
what we like
how we feel

Don't drink the water
same goes for you
fish

In the Pacific Northwest,
every time you tap the breaks
you kill a coho.

119,000,000 pill users
piss poison into the sea.

The Salish Sea
is a stew of chemicals,
measurable levels of
meth and
caffeine and
shit.

A man writes a letter
to the editor:
It's all pablum, he says,
Junk science,
Bureaucracy,

We're spent
as a people but
we keep at it.

The Feet in Our Seas

Water, on water, on bones,
every day, things disappear in the sea,
slip beneath its surface.

In the Salish Sea,
where the North Pacific dumps its surf,
feet wash up on beaches, feet still in their sneakers
sixteen so far
fourteen right and two left
perhaps they were from the tsunami
or maybe there is a serial killer,
or they came out of the Hecate Strait,
ground down in *clapotis* waves.

They are the feet of those missing from somewhere who,
years ago, were people who walked in time and place
on dry land. Now their bones travel currents
turning up in the mouths of dogs, who
greet their folk on the Western Rim.

The feet come from
China, or North Korea,
or Japan or Russia,
or the Philippines,
or British Columbia.
No one knows.
We only know what brine does to
those who once touched earth.

Our Pacific pushes on land
trimmed with conifers, making volcanoes,
kicking up five varieties of salmon
every child counts out on fingers—
Chum, Sockeye, King, Silver, Pink—

and throws up storms of fury.
We take what we can get,
we tell the Pacific we love it,
but the ocean does not speak
our love language.
The Pacific drowns us,
gives us feet.

The Heron

I.

In a metal box on the rocky shore of the Salish Sea, stands an object one meter high. Angled rings of light penetrate inner darkness, revealing a deep blue crown atop a still body with thin legs and a long, curved neck. *Ardea herodias.* The light passes and the shroud of darkness returns.

II.

The heronry on the point between two bays is battered by malevolent winds. The earth seems to tilt. A nest falls. Six baby herons lie broken on the forest floor as breakers lash the beach nearby, throwing up gnarled driftwood, rusted cans, and other jetsam. From these great birds, known for silence, comes a single, piercing scream that is drowned in the wind. Amid broken bones and tattered wings, there is a sole survivor.

III.

The sun, the moon, and the earth have aligned, gathered the tides, cast a shadow across the continent. The box is opened, the rescued heron steps out into the darkness, one ginger step after another, and rises to its full height. It surveys the bay, listens, listens, and listens. A sliver of golden light appears on the western edge of Padilla Bay as the moon releases the sun. The heron tenses, collects itself, and with a great snap of the wings takes flight from the shadows of the shore into the onrushing splendor of the sun.

The Sound of Mother at Rest

Have you seen the
place where we gathered
and stopped time?
The place where
the weeping willow we planted in '44
did its duty seventy-five years,
reaching, yearning, stretching
for ground? Where

Daughter,
with soil-stained hands
in her mother's garden:

rocks come out of the earth
one after another
this one a moon, she says,
that one a meteor,
this one a gas giant.

She takes off her shoes.
It's prickly, the grass, she says,
tosses hair from her eyes
catches a glimpse of what's above her—
clouds cross sky inland over islands and seas,

She repeats the names her mother taught her,
Fi-dal-go,
Rosario,
Juan de Fuca,
Salish,

Pacific.

She lays her head in Mother's lap,
listening for the sound of birds,
killdeer, plee o wee, wheep wheep,
naming them as her mother taught her.
She falls asleep.

Mother reclines,
spreads her arms,
reflects clouds from sunglasses
and breathes

the cycle of summer
unbroken,
gentle, but for
the sting of bees.

Until autumn,
we repeat the days.

Have you seen it?
It's a junkyard now,
all engine blocks,
rims, rusted doors.

The weeping willow is stacked
high in the yard, ready to burn.

A Western Sea

At the edge of western America,
with back turned to the sea,
islands in a sea of mud.
The shadow of a bird passes across the flats.
Looking up,
two birds in tandem,
moving north.
Wait, and the sea will return
with the tide, mixing
among pilings of rusted tinplate ruins,
reddish-brown circles ripple
toward the shore, wave by wave, with
all the rocks we threw in the sea
as kids returned to us
stained by the sea,
salted by a million tears
tossed and tumbled year upon year
sharpness smoothed and grounded
frosted blue and rounded,
like gemstones,
each fragment a narrative of creation, loss, and renewal
like a family that tells no stories and
as if by chance encounter with a touchstone
begins to talk, to let go the secrets of the past,
but thinks better of it, voices lost,
mixing with the sound of heavy stones
and sea glass, thrown into gentle rollers.

Again, we tumble.

Flood Stage, 1990

When, last, was my name on your lips?
Who reached to touch my shoulder,
wiped my brow after the hard rain
that raised the river?
Wasn't that you—you and me—filling
sandbags at the library, one after the other,
until downriver the dike broke?
We would have saved this town, we said,
if the earth hadn't done it for us
and flooded Fir Island while we
skipped up Snoqualmie Street,
drunk on fear and invincibility,
courage and wine.

We were young then.
Forever was a long time away. It was
a long time ago when I could still
call your face to my mind, a face whose
name I cannot remember.

Avon Cutoff

Out in the Avon Cutoff, a man thinks, *God, I guess you heard me, for I made it through the night.*

The screen door bangs out a minor key dirge-like rhythm. The wind blows through the willow. The river is up, running even with the dike. *They're probably sandbagging in town,* he thinks. He looks at his boots gathering dust, listens to the rain count out eighth notes on the roof. *Well, if it comes, it comes.* The hole in his sock chokes off the circulation in his big toe. Another day in bed. Another day in the bottle. Let the liquid find its level.

Old Hwy 99 South

I dig my hole,
You dig my grave,
Living who I am
While being who you are.

We are bound together,
Trapped inside a thought.
Who holds the gun?
Is there no time?

How far to go?
Ragged skin and
Worn-out bones
Trapped beneath the sky.

Who holds the sun
So far away from me?
You dig my hole and
I dig your grave.

Ghost Town, Population Three

Once, there was a man who sat on a stool outside
the old bar in Ghost Town.
Each afternoon, he played the harmonica until the sun set.
Then he would wipe the spittle off, put it in his shirt pocket,
button it, and look at the stars.
One day a government man came around
wanting to buy Ghost Town.
He had a paper in his pocket and asked to see the man.
An old man came out of the woods and disrobed.
He told Government Man,
I'm more comfortable this way.
They both listened to soft and euphonious harmonica music,
air pushing through comb and reed,
echoing through abandoned aluminum alleys,
floating out under the big sky
beyond Ghost Town, where
sound filled up the hollow bowl
where the copper used to be.

My Brother in Portugal

I called my brother in Portugal.
He lives in a small apartment in Guimarães.
I said,
> *Brother, how is life in Portugal?*

He replied, in Portuguese,
> *Eu não tenho um irmão.*

I did not understand and hung up.
> I miss my brother.

My Brother in Portugal, the Sequel

My brother in Portugal has two small dogs.
He bought them in Porto from a dead woman's son and
hauled them by car in two carriers to Guimarães.
They rocked to and fro and were sick in the back seat.

I called him yesterday and heard their yapping in the background.
I said,
> *Brother, how're your pups?*
He replied, in Portuguese,
> *Eu não tenho um irmão.*
I did not understand and hung up.
I long to tell my brother in Portugal all the things in my life
that he has missed.

A Germantown Scene

Lucky rear-ended Lover's car.
Just banged his baby, his prized GT, into the back of the old Buick.
He got out of the car and had a look.
He was all lank and leather from his motorcycle days—
He still tied his hair back
as if he didn't know it was all over.

Here comes Lover up the street
kicking her a box from the corner store.
If he was all lank then she was all long.
See those blonde locks flow?
She was on a string but that don't mean she can't be free.

Whole city on a string these days.
Pack your things, she said, *get on down the line.*
For the third time this week,
Lucky popped the trunk and tossed in a box.
All the cars on this street have dents.

I Knew You When

I.

She was a street hawk at
35th and Fremont.
She wore a
shock, shock, shock
collar, man kept her on a leash
straighten up fly right have a jolt now
she felt a twinge a little burn slight tingle and
numb.

She preaches his book near
the fingerpost at the center of the universe.
This way Xanadu, east of the sun
troll 2 blks, Lenin 1 block.
The Foundry 2.5 blks, silent,
mute, carved rock ruins of
different centuries and better days,
Glory! She preaches his book,

a testament to her man
she loves the man
she completes the man
she follows the man
It's not a cult, man, he is a
thin-ankle man
short athletic socks and combat boots man

she's on her corner spreading his faith:
      there's poor camps and tower cranes
      people packed in RVs, rumbles in the Jungle
      Amazonian spheres, number one on the west coast,
      Xanadu 2.0.

That's not what we fought for!

II.

He came north out of So-Cal, born of raw scrub,
wears a t-shirt and a bowl cut, leans on a bucket
against a building drinking Starbucks, scrolling
Tinder.
Going up Aurora
only one way in
and one way out
only one way in

and one way out
she is so thin
and he's thin too
he's a hype man
winding her up
he *sweats, sweats, sweats,* rubs
his chin.
Relax, he says, *it's art, man.*

III.

The sun is going down.
The street becomes neon.
I said to her, *I know you.*
She said, *Don't talk.*
She speaks her mind.
She says *Do you remember*
we went roller-skating
I could take the turn sharp but
you always went wide
do you remember
Wednesdays at the rink
All Skate/Couples Skate/Women Only/Re-verse
I knew you when you were young
before all this,
and you were scared.

She says to me, *I see you,* says,
there but for the grace of God, go I.

A Girl in the Chuckanuts

In afternoon sun after winter snow,
a girl runs on a farm above the bay at the edge of the Chuckanuts.
She runs, the sun drenches her,
she wears the colors of the rainbow on her jacket.
Her legs pump, boots crunch,
she's running up the farm lane now,
she's running with dogs.
She comes to the door of the cottage,
the dogs are circling her, barking, woofing.
They want to play.
She bangs on the door until she is exhausted.
She slumps to the ground
and the dogs lick at her face,
lap up her tears.

Waves turn over and over on the shore below.
For most of their stretch up the continent,
the Cascades keep their distance,
but in the Chuckanuts
they reach for the sea
and touch it.

Farm Dogs

Two old farm dogs put down on the same day.
Years and years together,
from pups to blindness,
no strength to meet death on their own time.

A young girl unsure,
thinking about crying,
she cries at thunder
but holding back now.

Old grandfather, hand at head
peering through sun,
she tries to comfort the old man.
Tells about lip gloss and
her preferred method of application.

He says to her, *What's the only cap you can't take off?*

The knee cap.

She blushes rose red.
He says, *two good loyal farm dogs*
buried beneath an elm tree
behind the farmhouse
on up a dirt road, one summer
by the Salish Sea.

Walking With Carver

I took Carver up the mountain in my pocket, as he took Machado before me, to a place where I could see the river empty into the bay. Carver took out Machado near a river and asked of nature what cannot be given. It's a bittersweet day, where to love in absence is to pull from a deep well of memory and find it dry, and I too ask of nature what cannot be given. What then was the last touch, the one beyond flesh, the one racing away, down the mountain, to where river becomes bay? What do I hear with eyes closed, Carver? Not the river, but I trust you will get the message, as Machado surely received yours, and I hope it is enough.

Metempsychosis

After Raymond Carver

On the phone, her granddaddy was telling her:

*It's at the oxbow. Near the steelhead hole. Head for the east county.
Go upriver toward the Cascades. Turn right off the highway at the last
big town. Go a bit south and peel off at the bridge where the water is
a deep emerald green. Follow the river going east again. Go past the
clear cuts on the ridges and the tumbledown gas station at Day Creek.
Go across them creeks: one creek, two creeks, three creeks. The one you
want is number sixteen. At the oxbow. You'll be someways up now but
not quite there. You've got some walking to do. Follow the trail through
the forest east northeast about a mile and there you'll see it. Some say
there's a man that done it. Others say it was the timber company.
I'd like to think it was some kind of mystery, an act of God or nature—
a bolt from the blue or maybe from giving up the ghost. Anyway, if you
know what yer looking for you'll see it. A tree that fell, split in two, a
century or century and a half ago, and birthed two stands of western
red cedar in straight lines, come together at a right angle. At the
oxbow, near the steelhead hole. It's there, if you know how to find it.
On east a here.*

Zeus

In the Salish Sea country,
gone gray beneath
the unnamed mountain, unknowing
the name the Salish gave it
the name the Spanish gave it
the name the British gave it
the name the settlers gave it
unknown.

Zeus wanders among gods, fallen,
bespectacled, bearded, forgiven
the yawns of tired folk in lowlight
bodies still warm,
who say good riddance,
after thirty years,
scarred, tattooed, the war of
the bodies is over,
the last hard inch won in
blood;
blood dries on
still moist ragged
scarred skin, flakes,
blown away
the bones remain
hollowed out bones in
the charnel house,
the bones of victors.

The ceasing of the constant
tearing rhythm of violence
builds anew the hopes for a lasting
peace, the wars of the bodies,
they are separate things,
the soul and the flesh,
so the believers tell me
in dark sanctuaries
candlelit, the chants of robed men,
pious women crawling up
steps on hands and knees, women
who cover their heads—

Zeus mingles
among us,
among tourists,
among pilgrims,

we light candles,
claim dominion
over the earth,
unknowing.

The gray gives way to blue.

Messianism

Sitting with Sasha
on a bench inside
the Church of St. Catherine
off Nevsky,

Lenin and Brezhnev sit idly
below us, bronzed, stiff, silent
in the basement pool,
drained,
not kitsch, the real thing,
the millenarian dream.

Sasha shows me the *Tanakh,* reads to
me from *The New Testament*
tells me about the gamblers and narcos
of Piter as he prepares
black bread with butter,
turning the knife's blade
one side to the other,
one side to the other.

Randall, please
your name is very difficult
to say in Russian—Randall,
he breaks the bread,
hands me a piece
crumbs falling to the floor

and speaks of Mashiach,
and of Yeshua,
prophesies the fall of America,
the turning of it to stone.

Please, Randall,
eat this bread
and let us ponder
the End of Days.

Ash Wednesday

In a boat near the Deadman Islands in Skagit Bay,
pulling in crab pots with Big Jim,
he was saying,

It was back in aught one. In the hay country east of the mountains.
There she was, elbow cocked at her side, cigarette in hand, smoke
trailing off east. She always did her hair up in a bun with a pencil in
the back like. So she's telling me about East Berlin and being followed
by the Stasi when she was in grad school and I have just gone dumb,
watching the earth come at her, just rolled right through her before it
come at me, sent us ass over tea kettle. I remember the sound of that
pencil rolling over cracked concrete with a cigarette trailing after,
spinning smoke. She come up on all fours, hair a mess, disheveled,
and I'm no better, I suppose, and she said, "Was that the Big One?"
She reached up and traced the cross of ash on my forehead.
Instinctively, I did the same to her. "I don't expect it was," I told her.
"We're still here." Anyways, I saw her yesterday at the rest stop in
Custer holding a sign that read, WILL SUFFERING EVER END?
We took each other in for a long moment and then we pretended not
to know one another. I reckon there's some things you don't forget.
Anyways.

Once a Coal Train Rumbles

There is a town in southern Finland with a castle on a hill. The castle is made of red brick, Kremlin-style. There is a moat around the castle. If you find it on Google maps, you can walk from the castle down a path to a lake. I had been talking to a friend in Helsinki last week, reminiscing about people we know and riding the tram around the city. I was thinking about this earlier tonight, while with some work friends who come from other places, at Bellingham Bay, watching the tide come in. A man skimboarded. The Alaskan Ferry headed out to sea. Kids threw rocks in the surf. The coal train rumbled along the coast to Cherry Point. All the places we'd been, here, now, together for the briefest moment in time. Warm, tilting into the sun, at peace.

An Abandoned Machine

There was his granny coming across the yard to him, her long bare feet making impressions in the grass. Those feet that carried her across the country in the 1940s when it seemed like all the Tar Heels in Appalachia came out of the Nantahala Forest and settled by the Western Sea in the Cascade foothills.

He'd like to have a patch of ground, dreamed of turning over soil so that it could be trod by giants and light-bringers like his granny, coming to say to a little one, *you hung the moon for me.*

But the earth shifted under him. He wandered through the lives of others, on bar stools and back roads, never quite getting to an idea you could call good. In his gut, he was tired. Then one day he was out on Fir Island on the way to Fish Town and in that golden Skagit light they call magic, he saw it. A machine with a sign on it: *For Sale.*

The machine sits on a country road between two curves. The curve in the easterly direction is covered in dried and fading blood from some catastrophic event involving livestock. Whether it was cows, pigs, or horses, no one remembered. They never did get the blood out of the macadam. A hundred yards on in the westerly direction sits a vigilant Virgin Mary, of marble, interceding for all those weary souls who, although coming into this world by accident or by chance, have scarred and stained the soils of the earth, in hopes that one day they too could say they left their mark on it. It was here in this place he began to clear the land.

To touch the muck at Turner's Bay or Similk Beach is to touch the remnants of volcanoes. It is the dissipated anger of the mountain Dakobed that threw its phyllite and glacial sediment into the rivers Sauk and Skagit, 6000 years ago. It is the silt from Dakobed and Kulshan that makes land in the bay, the land creeping west against the sea. The sea will have the final say in shaping the earth here. If you stand there long enough you can watch it happening, though most people do not notice. They look out over the bay and feel peace. What permanence can there be for the earth-mover and the plans of a man in the shadow of these giants?

When the Big Dark came that autumn, he took to bed, day after day, lost in reverie. Thought about the last day she lived there. He could hear her in the shower, weeping. Earlier, she said she didn't feel right, but it missed the part of his brain that still heard her. When she got out, he said,

I think we might ought to get a goat.

No.

We live on a farm though.

But we're not farmers.

Did you see the pileated woodpecker this morning?

I heard it.

And the gray horse kicked the big tan one today. Square in the ass.

They have names, and know 'em too.

Be nice to take care of something.

We're not getting a goat. They're escape artists. And nothing much holds your attention very long.

On the radio, a voice said, *Six days of rain coming.* He thought, *no sense in getting out of bed. No sense to it at all.*

He let the machine sit.

—

When the snow came that first winter on the farm, he had not been expecting it. Hadn't even thought about the possibility of winter out in the county. When the tree fell across the access road to the farm and cut the power, he was unprepared for living in a pre-modern world. The darkness defeated him, threatened to suffocate him, but the panic soon gave way to lethargy. He sat a good long while with nothing but socks between his feet and the chilled floor, failing to get the message his brain was sending him. It was telling him to get moving, and for God's sake get warm. Out on the bay, a Great Blue Heron crept along the shore. It put its beak in the water over and over, each time coming up empty.

As a boy he saw the mountain rush to the sea. He forgot what it felt like to feel that in his bones. Forgot there were people drowned in the mud. Forgot about the thousands of pyrolyzed firs and hemlocks shorn of deep, evergreen coats. It seemed like, after a heavy sigh, they all gave up the ghost and laid down to die. Nowadays when a low rumble comes from the movement of tracks across the earth, he keeps an eye on the mountain, but he doesn't know why.

Near the end of things, he moved the earth. One day and then another and another until the machine belched, burped, and lurched to a stop. You know the sound of a machine dying. The end of the Big Idea. He climbed down, had a look, wiped his brow. *Well, hell.* He stood there a long while thinking of small things in the silence, trying to get a handle on a life that's left him, until the sweat cooled and shivered him. He never did hear the sound the earth makes when it exhales, slow and steady, and takes back one small measure of what it is owed.

Day Labor

I.

In the car this morning, forty minutes northbound,
sixty minutes after the dispatch call,
dark until I saw the sun in Bellingham,
then hammers and staple guns and
the noise of cranes cabling booms and
Genies pushing buckets into the first blue sky
of day above oak trees aglow in autumnal hues.

Voices in Spanish, Russian, and English ring out
¡Ándale! ¡Órale! ¡Arriba!
Давай-давай пожалуйста
What's up, what's up!?
The bosses come out of the trailer in white hats
single file down the stairs, the bosses,
let's leave the bosses out of it.

II.

Its wetland, the mud is thick
the heron, stock-still in the retention pond,
surveys ducks that swim near, dipping beaks
into miasmic water.

It's my job to pick trash out of the creek that
feeds the pond: Beer cans, Styrofoam, shingles, chips, nails, a dozen
        orange
basketballs that bounded down from the court above,
the air slowly leaking out, a dozen orbs hissing gas among the weeds.

III.

It's appliance day: sleek new
refrigerators, dishwashers, stoves,
dryers and washers for
108 units; delivery made difficult by
aging hand trucks with fraying straps.

T says to E,
I was born in El Salvador too
T escaped war when he was two days old.
His mother and father dodged bombs from
safehouse to safehouse and bunker to bunker
until they reached Guatemala—his father played football and had
connections

E tells T what he missed:
born in a village where
his father knew many farmers but only a few soldados of the
Frente Farabundo Martí para la Liberación Nacional.

When the Mano Blanca drained the sea,
E heard screams in his dreams and
woke to familial, familiar, heads on stakes. His
father rose at three a.m. to take them down, so E would not see.
But these are things to which children bear witness, and so he saw
T and E, American citizens now, move refrigerators and talk about how
    much
they like the work, the simplicity of carrying things
up the stairs, in the shadow of Mount Baker, out of the shadow
of a past they do not share.

IV.

T is a prize-fighter who
works day labor between bouts.
He won $2000 in his last fight. At lunch
he asked me if we were close to a war like El Salvador
or if ideals were enough to preserve us.
He asked me if we lived in a closed universe,
if I thought we had souls or if we just turned
to dust upon death. *Just black, you know? No memories.*

T broke his hand in his last fight, it was worth $2000, for his kids.
He believes in ghosts. Do I?
I don't know, I see my mother in my dreams, I said.
I think you are a spiritual being, says T, *there's something
that connects us all. Stardust and Jesus, or whatever your god is.
My body is a vessel for the soul, I prepare it for
what is to come,* he says. *Moving refrigerators,
it's just something we have to do today.*

Principles of Construction Site Cleanup

No one will talk to a clean-up person except another clean-up person.
Together you may discuss the proper way to pick up nails

scattered across the pavement, the mud, the grass.
The answer: a magnet.

Any three clean-up persons may call themselves a crew.
provided they walk in step.

If four or more cleaners are on the crew,
one will think himself a boss,

think he knows more than the superintendent.
He will be bitter about his lot and run down the job.

He might get fired for pinching a tool belt or a knox box.

Let drywall stay as it lays if in pieces.
As dust is to dust, it will return to the earth.

Do not touch roofing debris.
There are laws about it, and

roofers have their own clean-up person who doubles as a gofer—
go for lunch, go for beer, go for weed, go.

The siders will call measures all day:
eight and a quarter strong, eight and a quarter shy.

Ruthless, they are paid by the foot;
they are experts in sabotage.

Elite cleaners work on high rise sites in the city where constant motion
        is required.
There is no time for contemplation. The clock is ticking:

One hour worked pays for parking,
the second hour worked goes for gas,

the third hour worked goes to the car prowler,
the fourth hour worked goes to the tax man,

the fifth hour worked goes to the bank for the car note,
the sixth hour of work goes to the landlord for the rent,

the seventh hour of work goes to Puget Power for the light.
After that, you can keep the rest, provided you have no debt.

You can save a little
if you take the bus.

You may be asked to relay a message of some concern
with all due dispatch to the foreman.

Deliver the message with clarity:
The dishwashers are plumbed wrong.

*It was eight and a quarter strong not
eight and a quarter shy,*

*the carpenter's gone AWOL,
OSHAs onsite.*

When a boss gives you direction, say loud and proud,
Yeah boss!

If a subcontractor asks you to clean up a mess, say
Do it your own damn self.

When the boss says you are unskilled labor,
says his nephew would do this for $10 an hour,

says it's what the market will bear,
says you ought to think about your choices in life,

say loud and proud, *Yeah, boss!*
Listen closely for the one moment in every day

when every hammer, saw, and drill, goes silent.
Listen how quiet it is.

Take pride in your role, always keep your trash can close, but
plot a revolution.

Ezra, Who Welds

Her whole life has been things tearing apart. To spite him she learned to strike—strike and hold the arc, flick and listen for the snap, stick, bend it quick, pull it free. She's a master of every weld: Butt welds, lap welds, and edge welds. Plug welds, T welds and strap joints. V welds and fillet welds, done in flat, vertical, and overhead positions. She carries the tools of her trade. Helmet, gloves, apron, electrode holder, hooks for the ground lead. Steel wire and scratch brush, a small chisel to clear slag. A box of soapstone crayons for marking on steel. Top hands defile her helmet, turn off her machine, and wish for her the Arc Eye. But she is careful and steady.

She dials in the current to 125 amperes, flips down her hood and strikes the arc. Awash in baptismal sparks, she guides the electrode through the weld. She feels safe, focused, protected, fusing things together. Stamping her initials into perfect, permanent welds, broken and cracked steel in reunion as mind is to body. Scarred, whole, sacred.

The Turf Farm

On the turf farm between the highways, setting stakes in the ground every eight feet. It's the same field my father drove a tractor in 60 years ago. Sun bakes dirt in skin. Bend, push, tie, set, stand, step, bendpushtiesetstandstep. Keep your mouth shut, pray, bend, push, tie, set, stand, step. Guy tells his life story, spent 30 days as an empath, doesn't eat fish, never in his life had rhubarb, been stabbed in the neck and lived, has a low opinion of women. *Shut up about that,* he's told. Never shuts up. Says, *I used to be a professional. Had a life in SoCal, near the beach. Had a reputation. We all used to be something,* he's told. Bend, push, tie, set, stand, step. Used to be like clockwork, tick-tock, reliable, now I'm day labor. Tells the boss, *you oughtta automate, get a machine to do this, oughta invent one.* Boss says they already have. *Why don't you have one?* Guy asks him. Boss says, *cuz we got you.* Bend, push, tie, set, stand, step. Every eight feet. Eventually, no one talks. No one drinks enough water. Ten hours later we all go home.

The Reefer in Lynden

A traveling crew comes to do a job at the reefer in Lynden. It is the one beyond the cemetery, and then the other cemetery, across from the cow pasture, near the border with Canada. The crew comes from Honduras, New York, Georgia. There are some locals and a tall guy who only says he's *from around*. They come to do this job in midsummer heat below the Garibaldi Ranges. One of these men shits on the outhouse floor.

A company man needed four thousand holes drilled in concrete and so we did it, hunched over our drills, hour after hour, amid a symphony of industrial terror. Drills in unison pulverize the smooth finish and render dust that piles in perfect circles around the sinking bit. Each revolution is a descent into madness, a private hell beyond salvation, where one's worst demons demand satisfaction. Relief breaks and breath returns when the bit strikes bottom and lasts until the trigger is pulled again. The crew boss repeats his watchword, *Forward*. And we go, inch by inch, into the last days of labor.

Puget Sound Refinery:
The Universe at the Point of Contraction

Hands gather in the dark December
on Contractor Row for shift-change. The refinery
hums, hisses, and rattles, steam vents from
the ground in great billows across roads and footpaths, like mist,
warm mist, poison mist, ripple-the-pant-leg mist, is that a
steam burn mist? Mist drifts through the yellow lights that dangle from
       pipe racks
and lamp posts on the units: Alky 1, Cat Cracker, Poly, the Boiler House,
the Coker, scorched, the killer Coker, it's killed fast and it's killed slow.
This refinery in all its modern, sublime beauty: industrial terror
lights up the Salish Sea this night, a shining city
on a hill, reflecting on calm, black water.
           They used to call it *Progress*.

In from the sea comes a low, thick layer of white cloud cover
over the supertankers out of Valdez arrayed in the bay,
encasing the refinery in a white dome, refracting yellow light,
the flame of the flare tower singes the bottom of clouds.
Weary groups of craftsmen from the night shift
shuffle silently towards the front gate, for home,
to lie down beside wives and girlfriends,
to leave thick, black, coke dust on white pillows,
they never get clean, it's in their hair, their lungs, their
caskets.

The morning crew passes through turnstiles,
badge reader beeping, tracking.
They trudge through gravel, dragging their
bodies along, stomping, kicking rocks,
kicking heat into their feet,
worn out already, the pre-dawn cold
rips through muscle, a hundred walking skeletons
who know how to turn a screw,
in their last solitary moments before
the shutdown begins, the turnaround,
the refit, 42 days,
13 days on, one off, if anyone is checking,
seven twelves and then six twelves and
repeat. Long enough to become unvoiced,
short-tempered, brain-addled, some men
will walk behind the smoke shack and cry,
they can't hear themselves think.

They are travelers, roustabouts, roughnecks,
Union men and women, OCAW! IUPIW!
If you are one of them, when
the Top Hand says you are one of them, then you are
Pork Chop, Knucklehead, Professor, there's

Bug, Pinky, Farmer, Daffy, Deputy Dog, and Doc, they are
sparkies and rod-busters, pipe-fitters and welders, civil men,
heavy equipment operators, they come out of the Army
and the Navy, out of the prisons and detoxes, they are
a crew—

In the single-wide trailer sit
twenty men and five women, cramped on dirty,
wooden benches between five wobbly plastic tables.
They are *gearing up,* getting into work boots,
strapping on tool belts. Some sit reclined
against the walls, smoking,
Lead man dragging on a cigarette,
blowing smoke through the hole where his teeth used to be,
puffs of white squares floating off above bowed heads
of Bible men forestalling the last temptations of fallen men,
praying off last night's tavern sins, keeping eyes low, averted
from the female fire watches removing the signs of
femininity, tying and tucking hair under hard hats,
slipping into oversize Nomex coveralls. Others
apply brand new stickers to their hard hats,
"Top Cat," "Sasquatch," "PSR 1995."

Frank,
a gaunt, broken man in his middle fifties,
starting all over again at the
bottom of the scale, the tool room manager,
sips coffee from a Styrofoam cup.
He is all geared up, in coveralls and hard-hat,
with oversize safety glasses over his broken spectacles.
He does not need to wear these things in the tool room,
but he wants to be prepared. He wants to get the call
to ride the sidestep pickup with the top men into the units.
Wants to pull hose and fire watch, tie the bowline,
send up wrenches on long ropes into the pipe rack,
he's been practicing, repeating *up through the rabbit hole,*
round the big tree; down through the rabbit hole and off
goes he, back in the hole—
He sits zazen on the bench and
holds the pose, shows the cracked yellow teeth
of a smile.

Frank arrives every morning and makes coffee,
hard, thick stuff that stains gullets and Styrofoam,
the way they did it up north in Alaska,
where your bones froze. He sits there dying
but no one likes him, he's a little "ducky,"
telling stories and more stories:
how he built that runway in Germany in '68 for Uncle Sam,
how he killed that bear in the Kenai in '73 and dragged it out
by himself, about putting in the pipeline on the North Slope in '76;
he is the hero of his own story, starts in on how

90

there are places on this earth where time does not exist.
In the desert, in caves, you have to have people, he says,
for time to exist, you have to have light. My time is older,
but we share this time because we share this light. Out there
under the bay, through the reflection, in the dark, is a place
on earth where time does not exist—

The foreman comes in and calls:
Let's make some gasoline!

Clean boots, crisp overalls, new gloves,
still sleepy, still thinking of the comfort of bed and
those they left there, they bend into the back of
early model Ford Rangers and Chevy stepside trucks, all
but Frank.

The cold gets into the cracks of fingers, water forms in the eyes
from the wind off the bay, the wind comes and comes, they sit
hunched, clutching knees, shoulder to shoulder,
coveralls, long johns, and tee-shirts
can't keep wind from reaching bone.

Everything feels slow, time is slow, no watches
on the unit, no phones, the whistle marks time, first break whistles,
lunch break whistles, second break whistles, knockoff-and-go-home
whistles,
whistles in the ears for years, even to the last breath
it sets the rhythm, never ceases, is present even at

the end of time.

Acknowledgments

I thank the editors of the following journals for publishing these poems:

CIRQUE: "The Last Days"
Eastern Iowa Review: "One Night Out West"
Terrain.org: "Theories of Translation," "Closed Doors at the End of
    the Universe," "Puget Sound Refinery: The Universe at the Point
    of Contraction"

Additionally, Raymond Carver's poem, "Waiting," from Raymond Carver's *All of Us: The Collected Poems* (New York: Vintage Contemporaries, 1996), serves as the loose inspiration for "Metempsychosis."

I offer my deepest thanks to my teacher, mentor, and friend Judyth Hill for opening the door to "the sweet life of poetry," and to Michael Daley for introducing a generation of students to poetry at Mount Vernon High School. I am ever grateful to the following readers and supporters: Danielle Kinsey, Kellie Nelson, Chris Nelson, Brendan Dailey, Laura Parker, Jason Dazey, Edna Adkins, Sean Dwyer, Dallas Jensen, James "Catfish" Jones, David C. Kane, Kenny Down, Will Cooley, Cami Ostman, Brenda Lovewell Bushey, Patty Smith, and the members of the Red Wheelbarrow Writers. I thank Kristi Carpenter for organizing the Skagit Watershed Master's program, the biologist Susan Wood for her poetic comments about photosynthesis, and Dr. David Beatty for his knowledge about salmon and watersheds. And to my father, Donald Dills, for 37 years of service to Puget Sound Refinery, and for understanding that Contractor Row was one stop, but not the final stop, on my journey.

About FutureCycle Press

FutureCycle Press is dedicated to publishing lasting English-language poetry in both print-on-demand and Kindle formats. Founded in 2007 by long-time independent editor/publishers and partners Diane Kistner and Robert S. King, the press was incorporated as a nonprofit in 2012. A number of our editors are distinguished poets and writers in their own right, and we have been actively involved in the small press movement going back to the early seventies.

Each year, we award the FutureCycle Poetry Book Prize and honorarium for the best original full-length volume of poetry we published that year. Introduced in 2013, proceeds from our Good Works projects are donated to charity. Our Selected Poems series highlights contemporary poets with a substantial body of work to their credit; with this series we strive to resurrect work that has had limited distribution and is now out of print.

We are dedicated to giving all of the authors we publish the care their work deserves, offering a catalog of the most diverse and distinguished work possible, and paying forward any earnings to fund more great books. All of our books are kept "alive" and available unless and until an author requests a title be taken out of print.

We've learned a few things about independent publishing over the years. We've also evolved a unique and resilient publishing model that allows us to focus mainly on vetting and preserving for posterity poetry collections of exceptional quality without becoming overwhelmed with bookkeeping and mailing, fundraising activities, or taxing editorial and production "bubbles." To find out more, come see us at futurecycle.org.

The FutureCycle Poetry Book Prize

All original, full-length poetry books published by FutureCycle Press in a given calendar year are considered for the annual FutureCycle Poetry Book Prize. This allows us to consider each submission on its own merits, outside of the context of a traditional contest. Too, the judges see the finished book, which will have benefitted from the beautiful book design and strong editorial gloss we are famous for.

The book ranked the best in judging is announced as the prize-winner in January of the subsequent year. There is no fixed monetary award; instead, the winning poet receives an honorarium of 20% of the total net royalties from all poetry books and chapbooks the press sold online in the year the winning book was published. The winner is also accorded the honor of being on the panel of judges for the next year's competition; all judges receive copies of the contending books to keep for their personal library.

www.ingramcontent.com/pod-product-compliance
Lightning Source LLC
Chambersburg PA
CBHW070003100426
42741CB00012B/3111